Team Spirit

THE NEW YORK GIANTS

BY

MARK STEWART

Content Consultant
Jason Aikens
Collections Curator
The Professional Football Hall of Fame

NORWOOD HOUSE PRESS

CHICAGO, ILLINOIS

Norwood House Press
P.O. Box 316598
Chicago, Illinois 60631

For information regarding Norwood House Press, please visit our website at:
www.norwoodhousepress.com or call 866-565-2900.

PHOTO CREDITS:
All photos courtesy of AP Images—AP/Wide World Photos, Inc. except the following:
Author's Collection (6 & 30); Bowman Gum Co. (14 & 21 top);
National Chicle (16); Topps, Inc. (20, 21 bottom, 26, 34 left,
35 top and bottom left, 37, 40 bottom, 41 both & 43);
John Klein (22 & 23 top); Petersen Publishing Company (34 right);
Black Book Archives (35 top right); CoolChooChoo (40 top).
Special thanks to Topps, Inc.

Editor: Mike Kennedy
Associate Editor: Brian Fitzgerald
Designer: Ron Jaffe
Project Management: Black Book Partners, LLC.
Special thanks to: Fred King and Jeff Malanga

LIBRARY OF CONGRESS CATALOGING-IN-PUBLICATION DATA

Stewart, Mark, 1960-
    The New York Giants / by Mark Stewart ; content consultant Jason Aikens.
        p. cm. -- (Team spirit)
    Summary: "Presents the history, accomplishments and key personalities of
the New York Giants football team. Includes timelines, quotes, maps,
glossary and websites"--Provided by publisher.
    Includes bibliographical references and index.
    ISBN-13: 978-1-59953-133-5 (library edition : alk. paper)
    ISBN-10: 1-59953-133-X (library edition : alk. paper)
    1. New York Giants (Football team)--History--Juvenile literature. I.
Aikens, Jason. II. Title.
GV956.N4S85 2008
796.332'64097471--dc22
                                                                2007007483

COVER PHOTO: Dhani Jones celebrates a big play during the 2002 season by leaping into the arms of Michael Barrow.

Table of Contents

SPORTS WORDS & VOCABULARY WORDS: In this book, you will find many words that are new to you. You may also see familiar words used in new ways. The glossary on page 46 gives the meanings of football words, as well as "everyday" words that have special football meanings. These words appear in **bold type** throughout the book. The glossary on page 47 gives the meanings of vocabulary words that are not related to football. They appear in ***bold italic type*** throughout the book.

Meet the Giants

A hard tackle, a crunching **block**, a great run, a fingertip catch—these are the "calling cards" of the New York Giants. The Giants are the fourth-oldest team in the **National Football League (NFL)**. They are also one of the great success stories in American sports. Win or lose, they are *cherished* by their fans.

When you wear the Giants uniform, it not only means playing in front of huge crowds. It means huge crowds in the locker room, too. No NFL team is covered by more newspaper, magazine, radio, television, and Internet reporters. No players spend more time in the spotlight.

This book tells the story of the Giants. For more than 80 seasons, they have made history and witnessed history. They have played in some of football's biggest games and found some of its brightest stars. The team is as much a part of the New York metropolitan area as the Empire State Building or the George Washington Bridge. And why not? The Giants were there first!

Jeremy Shockey gives Michael Strahan a pat on the back as the defense comes off the field. The Giants are at their best when they stop opponents from moving the football.

Way Back When

More than 17 million fans will buy tickets for NFL games this season. In the early days of the league, teams often drew only a few hundred spectators for a single game. That is why many New Yorkers were surprised in 1925 when Tim Mara bought an NFL team. Mara was a famous gambler and *sports promoter*, but the odds were clearly against him.

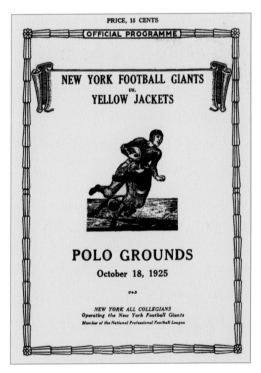

Mara's Giants had a good team in their first season, though not many people noticed. That was until the Chicago Bears came to town in December with their new star, Red Grange. More than 70,000 fans turned out to watch the game. Mara used the profits from that contest to find top players. Two seasons later, in 1927, the Giants were NFL champions.

The Giants had a great defense during their early years, thanks to **linemen** Steve Owen and Cal Hubbard. As the 1930s began,

LEFT: A program from the team's first home game in 1925.
RIGHT: Frank Gifford quickly changes direction against an enemy defender.

the Giants became known for their great offense. They had two of the NFL's top passers, Benny Friedman and Harry Newman, plus running back Ken Strong and receiver Red Badgro. New York's best player during this era was Mel Hein. He was the only offensive lineman ever to be named the NFL's **Most Valuable Player (MVP)**.

With Owen now coaching the team, the Giants won the championship in 1934 and 1938. He led the Giants to four more **NFL Championship** games between 1939 and 1946, but they lost each time. Tuffy Leemans, Ward Cuff, Monk Edwards, and Len Younce starred for those teams.

During the 1950s and early 1960s, the Giants were the NFL's most glamorous team. **Professional** football was growing in popularity, and New York had players with great skill and personality. The stars on offense were Charley Conerly, Frank Gifford, Don Heinrich, Alex Webster, Y.A. Tittle, Kyle Rote, and Roosevelt Brown.

Their amazing defense was led by Andy Robustelli, Emlen Tunnell, Sam Huff, Rosey Grier, Dick Modzelewski, and Jimmy Patton. From 1956 to 1963, the Giants played for the NFL Championship six times.

These glory years were followed by two *decades* of hardship. Some good players wore the Giants uniform during this time, including Spider Lockhart, Pete Gogolak, Fran Tarkenton, Ron Johnson, and Brad Van Pelt. Even so, from 1964 to 1983, the Giants had just three winning seasons.

Things finally changed when Bill Parcells became New York's coach. He rebuilt the Giants into a winning team with a defense that featured great linebackers such as Lawrence Taylor, Harry Carson, and Carl Banks. His quarterback, Phil Simms, also developed into a star. Parcells surrounded Simms with tough players who rose to the challenge in big games, including Joe Morris and Mark Bavaro. The Giants won two **Super Bowls** under Parcells. They have been one of the NFL's best teams ever since.

LEFT: Erik Howard raises his hands to congratulate Lawrence Taylor after the Giants sacked John Elway of the Denver Broncos in his own end zone during Super Bowl XXI. **ABOVE**: Phil Simms and Bill Parcells

The Team Today

Each season, the Giants try to build their team around a strong defense. The more difficult it is for an opponent to make first downs and score points, the more opportunities New York's offense will have to win. In recent years, the "Big Blue" defense has been **anchored** by Michael Strahan and Osi Umenyiora. However, it is teamwork—not stars—that makes the defense tough.

For leadership, the Giants have often looked to their quarterbacks. They do not ask them to be superstars. Rather, New York's quarterbacks must understand the best way to blend the skills of their teammates. In 2004, the Giants traded for Eli Manning. They believed he could be that kind of leader.

Manning began his career with **veterans** Tiki Barber and Amani Toomer in the huddle. The lessons he learned from those players will one day be passed on to future teammates. This is how it has been done for many decades in New York. This is the heart of "Giants football."

Eli Manning spots a change in the defense as he prepares to take a snap. The young quarterback gained important experience in his first few seasons with the Giants.

Home Turf

The first field in Giants history was the Polo Grounds in uptown Manhattan. In 1956, the team moved across the Harlem River to Yankee Stadium, in the Bronx. The Giants stayed there until 1973, when the stadium was **renovated**. After two seasons at the Yale Bowl in New Haven, Connecticut, they played at Shea Stadium, the home of the New York Mets baseball team.

In 1976, the team moved into Giants Stadium, which was built for them in the New Jersey Meadowlands, a few miles from New York City. In 1984, the New York Jets began playing there, too. In 2005, the Giants announced plans to build a new stadium in the Meadowlands Sports Complex.

BY THE NUMBERS

- *There are 80,242 seats for football in Giants Stadium.*
- *In 2005, the New Orleans Saints were the "home" team when they played the Giants in Giants Stadium. The Saints' stadium could not be used because of damage done to it by Hurricane Katrina.*
- *The largest crowd ever in Giants Stadium was 82,948. They were there to see Pope John Paul II.*
- *Giants Stadium hosted six soccer games during the 1994 World Cup.*

Fans gather in Giants Stadium in 1987 for a celebration to honor the team's first Super Bowl victory.

Dressed for Success

The color blue has always been a part of the Giants' uniform. Red, white, and gray have also been important team colors. For most of their history, the Giants have worn dark uniforms at home and white on the road. They wore red jerseys during the 1950s. In 2005, the team brought these uniforms back for their road games. The Giants have worn blue helmets for much of their history. They added a lowercase "ny" during the early 1960s.

In 1975, the Giants changed their uniform from head to toe. The new style kept the same colors but had a more modern look, with bolder stripes on the helmet, jersey, pants, and socks. When the team moved to New Jersey, the old helmet *logo* was replaced by the word "GIANTS." The team later went back to its *classic* "ny" helmet design.

Charley Conerly fires a pass in the team's uniform from 1950.

UNIFORM BASICS

The football uniform has three important parts—
- Helmet
- Jersey
- Pants

Helmets used to be made out of leather, and they did not have facemasks—ouch! Today, helmets are made of super-strong plastic. The uniform top, or jersey, is made of thick fabric. It fits snugly around a player so that tacklers cannot grab it and pull him down. The pants come down just over the knees.

10

There is a lot more to a football uniform than what you see on the outside. Air can be pumped inside the helmet to give it a snug, padded fit. The jersey covers shoulder pads, and sometimes a rib protector called a flak jacket. The pants include pads that protect the hips, thighs, *tailbone*, and knees.

Football teams have two sets of uniforms—one dark and one light. This makes it easier to tell two teams apart on the field. Almost all teams wear their dark uniforms at home and their light ones on the road.

Brandon Jacobs scores a touchdown in the team's 2006 home uniform.

We Won!

The Giants won their first championship in 1927. Back then, there was no NFL Championship game. The team that finished in first place was simply declared the winner for the year. The Giants won the title with defense. They allowed only 20 points in 13 games.

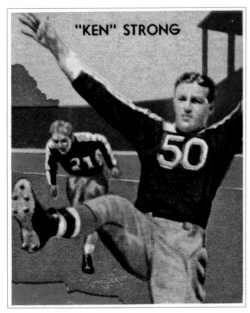

"KEN" STRONG

The Giants faced the Chicago Bears in the NFL's first two championship games, in 1933 and 1934. The Giants lost the first meeting but won the next one. This game was played on an icy field in New York. The Giants trailed by 10 points in the fourth quarter, but Ken Strong and Ed Danowski led a great comeback. New York earned a 30–13 victory.

In 1938, the Giants won their third title when they beat the Green Bay Packers 23–17. New York blocked two punts, and Hank Soar made a leaping catch on a long pass from Danowski for the winning touchdown.

The Giants did not wear the NFL crown again until 1956, when they beat the Bears again. That season, the Giants had one of the best teams ever. Against Chicago, Frank Gifford, Alex Webster, and Mel Triplett scored four touchdowns on offense. The big story, however, was New York's defense, which completely **dominated** the Bears. The Giants won 47–7.

The Giants played for the NFL Championship five times from 1958 to 1963 but lost each time. Their 1958 meeting with the Baltimore Colts was one of the most exciting games ever played. The Giants lost 23–17 in the NFL's first **overtime** game.

The Giants did not finish in first place again until 1986, when they won the **National Football Conference (NFC) Eastern Division** title. That team, led by quarterback Phil Simms and linebacker Lawrence Taylor, whipped the San Francisco 49ers and Washington Redskins in the **playoffs**. New York then defeated the Denver Broncos 39–20 in Super Bowl XXI. Simms played the best game of his life, and Carl Banks topped New York's hard-hitting linebackers with 10 tackles.

LEFT: Ken Strong, one of the team's stars during the 1930s.
ABOVE: Shirtless Charley Conerly throws his arm around Frank Gifford after New York's championship in 1956.

The Giants won their second Super Bowl four years later. That championship—the club's sixth—did not come easily. The team lost three of its last six games and limped into the playoffs without Simms. Jeff Hostetler did a good job in his place, but New York fell behind San Francisco in the NFC Championship game. With time running out and the 49ers moving down the field on offense, the Giants knocked the ball loose, and Taylor recovered the **fumble**. Moments later, Matt Bahr kicked the winning **field goal**.

One week later, in Super Bowl XXV, the Giants played the Buffalo Bills in a game that was close and exciting from beginning to end. Bahr booted a field goal to give the Giants a 20–19 lead in the fourth quarter. The Bills, however, had a chance to win on the game's last play with a field goal of their own. Millions of football fans held their breath as Scott Norwood boomed a kick from 47 yards away. The ball curved to the right at the last moment, and the kick was no good. The Giants were champions again!

LEFT: Phil Simms celebrates one of his three touchdown passes during Super Bowl XXI.   **ABOVE**: Lawrence Taylor and Carl Banks give Bill Parcells a victory ride.

Go-To Guys

To be a true star in the NFL, you need more than fast feet and a big body. You have to be a "go-to guy"—someone the coach wants on the field at the end of a big game. Giants fans have had a lot to cheer about over the years, including these great stars …

THE PIONEERS

MEL HEIN   Center/Linebacker

• BORN: 8/22/1909 • DIED: 1/31/1992 • PLAYED FOR TEAM: 1931 TO 1945

A great blocker and tackler, Mel Hein was one of football's most athletic players. He was named the NFL's best center from 1933 to 1940 and was league MVP in 1938.

CHUCK CONERLY
QUARTERBACK   NEW YORK GIANTS

CHARLEY CONERLY   Quarterback

• BORN: 9/19/1921 • DIED: 2/13/1996
• PLAYED FOR TEAM: 1948 TO 1961

Charley Conerly was booed so often by the New York fans in the early 1950s that he almost retired. Coach Jim Lee Howell talked him into coming back, and Conerly led the Giants to the NFL Championship. In 1959, Conerly was the league's top-rated passer and its MVP.

FRANK GIFFORD — Running Back/Receiver

- BORN: 8/16/1930
- PLAYED FOR TEAM: 1952 TO 1960 & 1962 TO 1964

Frank Gifford was the most *versatile* player in Giants history. He was a good runner and receiver, an accurate passer, and an excellent pass defender. Gifford was so talented that he could even kick field goals.

SAM HUFF — Linebacker

- BORN: 10/4/1934 • PLAYED FOR TEAM: 1956 TO 1963

Sam Huff was a great leader and fierce middle linebacker with amazing instincts. No matter where the ball was, he always seemed to be around it. The Giants played in six NFL Championship games during his eight years on the team.

Y.A. TITTLE — Quarterback

- BORN: 10/24/1926 • PLAYED FOR TEAM: 1961 TO 1964

New York fans thought 34-year-old Y.A. Tittle was done when he joined the team. Tittle shocked them by becoming the league's best passer and leading the Giants to the NFL Championship game three years in a row. In 1963, he set an NFL record with 36 touchdown passes.

LEFT: Charley Conerly
TOP RIGHT: Frank Gifford
BOTTOM RIGHT: Sam Huff

MODERN STARS

HARRY CARSON   Linebacker

• BORN: 11/26/1953   • PLAYED FOR TEAM: 1976 TO 1988

Harry Carson was one of the strongest linebackers in history. On running plays, he sometimes hit the player blocking him so hard that he flew backwards into the ball carrier, knocking both to the ground! Carson was named to the **Pro Bowl** every year from 1982 to 1988.

PHIL SIMMS   Quarterback

• BORN: 11/3/1954   • PLAYED FOR TEAM: 1979 TO 1993

When Phil Simms was **drafted** out of tiny Morehead State University, every fan in New York asked the same question: "Phil who?" When

Simms retired, he owned almost every team passing record. Simms was a great leader and strong passer who involved all of his teammates in the game.

LAWRENCE TAYLOR   Linebacker

• BORN: 2/4/1959

• PLAYED FOR TEAM: 1981 TO 1993

Along with Carson and Carl Banks, Lawrence Taylor formed one of the best linebacking crews in history. "L.T." was like a human wrecking ball. He was so fast and aggressive—and so unpredictable—that opponents had to change their **playbook** when they faced the Giants.

MICHAEL STRAHAN   Defensive Lineman

• BORN: 11/21/1971   • FIRST SEASON WITH TEAM: 1993

When Michael Strahan joined the Giants, they thought he would make a good linebacker. Once he moved to defensive end, they saw his true greatness. Strahan led the NFL in sacks in 2001 and 2003.

TIKI BARBER   Running Back

• BORN: 4/7/1975   • PLAYED FOR TEAM: 1997 TO 2006

Tiki Barber was a quick, powerful runner who could go up the middle, around the end, or catch short passes for big gains. In his final regular-season game, he ran for 234 yards to set a team record. Barber was just the third player in NFL history with 10,000 rushing yards and 5,000 receiving yards.

ELI MANNING   Quarterback

• BORN: 1/3/1981   • FIRST SEASON WITH TEAM: 2004

The Giants traded for Eli Manning after the San Diego Chargers chose him first in the 2004 **NFL draft**. In his first full year as a starter, he threw for more yards than his brother Peyton and tied for the NFC lead with 24 touchdown passes.

23

On the Sidelines

The Giants have had many great coaches. Steve Owen led the team to eight first-place finishes during the 1930s and 1940s. In his 23 years on the sidelines, Owen became known as a defensive genius. Jim Lee Howell followed Owen and assembled a great team that featured a high-scoring offense.

The Giants had other good coaches over the years, including Allie Sherman, Dan Reeves, Jim Fassel, and Tom Coughlin. Their best in recent years was Bill Parcells. He was the team's defensive coordinator for two years before he became the head coach in 1983. Parcells demanded that his players be in great shape and that they play hard and play smart. He led the Giants to victory in two Super Bowls.

Through all of the Giants' ups and downs, there was one person who was always on the sidelines—and always there as a friend for the players. Tim Mara's son Wellington worked as a water boy for the team in the 1920s and eventually became the owner. When he died in 2006, everyone in the NFL mourned his passing.

The beloved Wellington Mara chats with one of New York's defensive stars, Jason Sehorn, prior to Super Bowl XXXV.

One Great Day

When the Giants took the field for Super Bowl XXI, they hoped to win their first championship in 30 seasons. New York had a fast and furious defense, good special teams, and a powerful offense. The Giants' leader was their quarterback, Phil

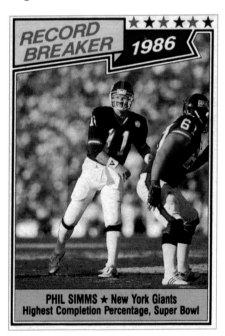

RECORD BREAKER 1986

PHIL SIMMS ★ New York Giants
Highest Completion Percentage, Super Bowl

Simms. For Simms, it had been a bumpy road to the Super Bowl.

When the team drafted him in 1979, many New York fans were angry. They had never heard of Simms, who played for a small college in Kentucky. During his first few years with the Giants, he was frequently injured, booed, and **benched**. Simms never lost his confidence, and the experience made him an amazing competitor.

The Denver Broncos found out just how amazing in January 1987. As Simms warmed up before the game, he had a big smile on his face. He told his teammates, "I've got it today!"

Simms probed and prodded the Denver defense in the first half, looking for its weaknesses. He passed for a touchdown, while the New York defense kept the Broncos in check. In the second half, Simms was practically perfect. The Broncos could not stop him. At one point, he completed 10 passes in a row. Simms threw touchdowns to Mark Bavaro and Phil McConkey, and led the Giants to two other touchdowns and a field goal. The final score was 39–20.

After the game, Simms could hardly believe his own numbers. He had attempted 25 passes and completed 22, including three touchdowns. The quarterback who could do nothing right when he came to New York could do no wrong on this day. "After all I've taken over the years," he said, "this makes everything worth it."

Legend Has It

Which Giant was the subject of a prize-winning photo?

LEGEND HAS IT that Y.A. Tittle was. After the Giants went to the NFL Championship game in 1963, age and injuries

caught up to the team. They won only twice in 1964. In a game against the Pittsburgh Steelers, Tittle was knocked to the ground again and again. A photo was taken of him kneeling, dazed and bloodied, in his own end zone. It seemed to tell the sad story of how far the team had fallen. More than 40 years later, the picture of Tittle is still one of football's most famous.

ABOVE: This picture of Y.A. Tittle is one of the most famous in sports.
RIGHT: Gotcha! Harry Carson—disguised in a yellow security jacket—showers Bill Parcells with Gatorade.

Was the football term "Red Dog" started by the Giants?

LEGEND HAS IT that it was. "Red Dog" is another name for a blitz—a surprise play when the defensive team sends extra pass rushers across the line. It was named for Don "Red" Ettinger, who played defense for the Giants. Ettinger once explained that his job was to "dog" the quarterback on this play. The Giants started calling their blitz "Red Dog" and the name just caught on.

Who started the NFL's "victory shower" celebration?

LEGEND HAS IT that Giants **nose tackle** Jim Burt did. But it was teammate Harry Carson who turned the victory shower into a football *tradition*. Burt, who spent eight seasons with the Giants, doused coach Bill Parcells for the first time after a win by the team in 1985. Carson loved the idea and took the lead on all future celebrations. Sometimes, he would even disguise himself on the sidelines so Parcells would not see him coming. Today, every football coach expects to get wet after a big win.

It Really Happened

When the Giants took the field for the 1934 NFL Championship against the Chicago Bears, there was not much field to see. A winter storm in New York had covered the grass at the Polo Grounds with a slick glaze of ice. Coach Steve Owen had no idea how his team would run its plays or tackle Bronko Nagurski, the Bears' powerful running back. Metal cleats would be useless on this day.

New York's star receiver, Ray Flaherty, suggested that the team wear basketball shoes. Owen liked the idea, but it was Sunday and every sporting goods store in the city was closed. The coach did not give up. He sent the team's equipment manager, Abe Cohen, to the local colleges looking for rubber-soled shoes.

Meanwhile, the Bears bullied and **brutalized** the Giants in the first half of their game. New York played bravely and allowed Chicago only 10 points, but the team was exhausted by halftime. Hope was slipping away when suddenly Cohen burst into the

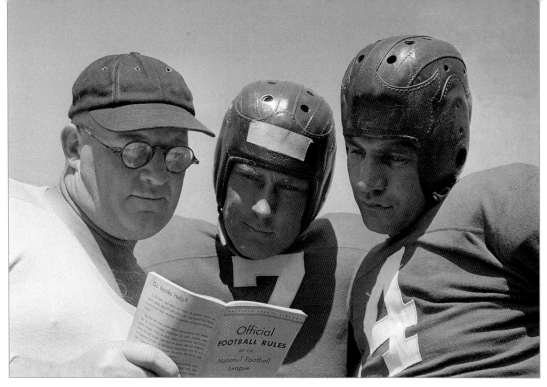

locker room with nine pairs of sneakers. He had found them in the gym at Manhattan College.

It took the Giants a while to get used to their new footwear. But once they did, their fakes and cuts left the Bears slipping and sliding all over the field. The Giants scored 27 points in the fourth quarter and won 30–13. Forever after, New York fans called this the "Sneaker Game."

When Manhattan's basketball coach looked at the torn and tattered sneakers after the game, he joked, "I'm glad our shoes did the Giants some good … the question is, did the Giants do our shoes any good?"

LEFT: In the 1930s, Giants fans supported their team by wearing buttons like this one.   **ABOVE**: Steve Owen goes over the NFL rule book with Mel Hein and Ken Strong, two of his stars in 1934. Nothing in it said players could not wear sneakers.

Team Spirit

Few places in the NFL have as much energy and excitement as Giants Stadium on game day. New York football fans follow the game closely, and their mood swings up and down with each play. When "Big Blue" scores, the noise can be *deafening*. If the fans think a player or coach is not doing his best, they let him know about it!

For some fans, just holding a Giants ticket is a thrill. The team's games have been sold out since Giants Stadium opened, and thousands of people are on the waiting list for **season tickets**. Many families have had seats since the 1960s. They have followed the team from the Bronx to Connecticut to Queens to New Jersey.

Giants fans like to think of themselves as "old school." They come to watch football, not mascots and cheerleaders. They are very knowledgeable about the sport and its history, and they study and discuss the visiting team before each game. Above all else, Giants fans are dedicated. Even when the team plays in driving rain or in a snowstorm, the stands are filled.

Giants fans get ready for their meeting with the Baltimore Ravens in Super Bowl XXXV.

Timeline

In this timeline, each Super Bowl is listed under the year it was played. Remember that the Super Bowl is held early in the year and is actually part of the previous season. For example, Super Bowl XLI was played on February 4th, 2007, but it was the championship of the 2006 NFL season.

1925
The Giants join the NFL.

1956
The Giants win their fourth NFL Championship.

1929
Benny Friedman sets an NFL record with 20 touchdown passes.

1934
The Giants win the NFL title in the famous "Sneaker Game."

1963
MVP Y.A. Tittle leads the Giants to their third division title in a row.

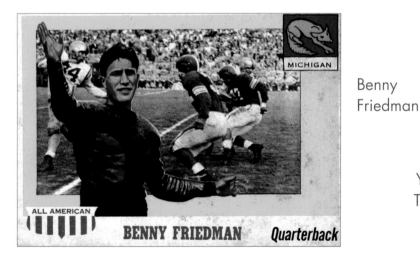

Benny Friedman

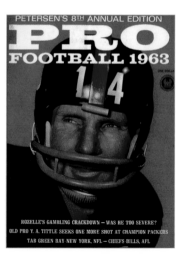

Y.A. Tittle

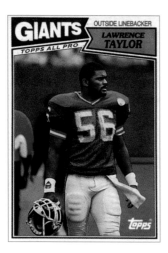

Lawrence
Taylor

Tiki
Barber

1981
Lawrence Taylor is
named **All-Pro** in
his rookie year.

1991
The Giants win
their second
Super Bowl.

2005
Tiki Barber leads the
NFL in **total yards** for
the second year in a row.

1976
Giants Stadium
opens.

1987
The Giants win their
first Super Bowl.

2002
Amani Toomer sets team
records with 82 catches
for 1,343 yards.

Mark Bavaro,
a star for
the Giants
in the 1980s.

Amani
Toomer

Fun Facts

AUTHOR! AUTHOR!

In 2005, Tiki Barber and his twin brother Ronde published a children's book entitled *Game Day*.

JUST FOR KICKS

In 1983, Ali Haji-Sheikh of the Giants established a record for field goals in a season. He finished the year with 35.

TOUGH GUY

Mel Hein played center and linebacker for the Giants for 15 seasons. In all those years, he only called timeout once—to push his own broken nose back into place.

IRON MAN

In 2005, Jeff Feagles of the Giants set an NFL record when he played in his 283rd game in a row.

A REAL HERO

Rosey Grier was known for chasing down running backs when he played for the Giants in the 1950s. In 1968, Grier caught Sirhan Sirhan, the man who *assassinated* Senator Robert Kennedy. Grier grabbed Sirhan and jammed his thumb behind the trigger of Sirhan's gun to prevent him from firing again.

MR. 200

Gene "Choo Choo" Roberts, a running back for the Giants, caught four passes for 201 yards against the Chicago Bears in a 1949 game. Three weeks later, he caught seven passes against the Green Bay Packers and gained 212 yards. He is the only running back in history with two 200-yard receiving days.

TRUE VALUE

When Lawrence Taylor was named NFL MVP in 1986, it was just the fourth time in history that a defensive player won the award.

TOP LEFT: Ronde and Tiki Barber
BOTTOM LEFT: Jeff Feagles   **ABOVE**: Rosey Grier

Talking Football

"Guys like Charley Conerly, Y.A. Tittle, and Rosie Brown were truly my brothers during those years of frozen fields, broken bones, and championship triumphs."

—Frank Gifford, on the feeling of family among the Giants in the 1950s and 1960s

"My entire life has been spent thinking about this game."

—Bill Parcells, on his dedication to coaching

"I hate to lose. Even at checkers."

—Jeremy Shockey, on the attitude he brought to the Giants

"There has always been—and will be—a Lawrence Taylor. But without the fans, there would have never been an L.T."

—Lawrence Taylor, on his close relationship with the New York fans

ABOVE: Jeremy Shockey
RIGHT: Tiki Barber laughs with students during a school visit.

"I've always taken pride in being a great student, besides being
a great athlete."

    —*Tiki Barber, on the importance of doing well in school*

"When I came to New York, the big stars in town were the
defensive players ... By the time I retired, the fans loved
the offensive part of the game."

    —*Y.A. Tittle, on how Giants fans came to appreciate offense*

"With the game on the line, I want the ball in my hands."

    —*Eli Manning, on being a confident quarterback*

"The NFL is about winning games late."

    —*Phil Simms, on playing your best in the fourth quarter*

For the Record

T he great Giants teams and players have left their marks on the record books. These are the "best of the best" …

Mel Hein

Phil Simms

GIANTS AWARD WINNERS

WINNER	AWARD	YEAR
Mel Hein	NFL Most Valuable Player	1938
Frank Gifford	Pro Bowl co-MVP	1959
Charley Conerly	NFL Most Valuable Player	1959
Allie Sherman	NFL Coach of the Year	1961
Allie Sherman	NFL Coach of the Year	1962
Y.A. Tittle	NFL Most Valuable Player	1963
Lawrence Taylor	NFL Defensive Rookie of the Year	1981
Lawrence Taylor	NFL Defensive Player of the Year	1981
Lawrence Taylor	NFL Defensive Player of the Year	1982
Phil Simms	Pro Bowl MVP	1986
Lawrence Taylor	NFL Defensive Player of the Year	1986
Bill Parcells	NFL Coach of the Year	1986
Lawrence Taylor	NFL Most Valuable Player	1986
Phil Simms	Super Bowl XXI MVP	1987
Ottis Anderson	Super Bowl XXV MVP	1991
Dan Reeves	NFL Coach of the Year	1993
Jim Fassel	NFL Coach of the Year	1997
Michael Strahan	NFL Defensive Player of the Year	2001

GIANTS ACHIEVEMENTS

ACHIEVEMENT	YEAR
NFL Champions	1927
NFL Eastern Division Champions	1933
NFL Eastern Division Champions	1934
NFL Champions	1934
NFL Eastern Division Champions	1935
NFL Eastern Division Champions	1938
NFL Champions	1938
NFL Eastern Division Champions	1939
NFL Eastern Division Champions	1941
NFL Eastern Division Champions	1944
NFL Eastern Division Champions	1946
NFL Eastern Division Champions	1956
NFL Champions	1956
NFL Eastern Division Champions	1958
NFL Eastern Division Champions	1959
NFL Eastern Conference Champions	1961
NFL Eastern Conference Champions	1962
NFL Eastern Conference Champions	1963
NFC East Champions	1986
NFC Champions	1986
Super Bowl XXI Champions	1986*
NFC East Champions	1989
NFC East Champions	1990
NFC Champions	1990
Super Bowl XXV Champions	1990
NFC East Champions	1997
NFC East Champions	2000
NFC Champions	2000
NFC East Champions	2005

*Super Bowls are played early the following year,
   but the game is counted as the championship of this season.*

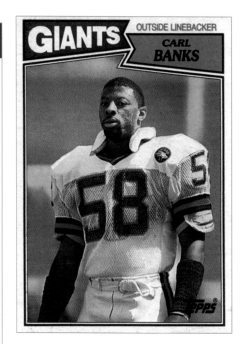

Carl Banks and Harry Carson, two of New York's heroes from Super Bowl XXI.

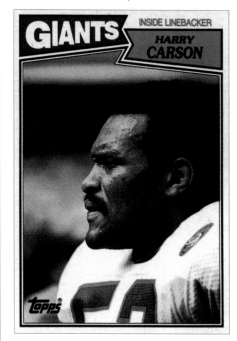

Pinpoints

The history of a football team is made up of many smaller stories. These stories take place all over the map—not just in the city a team calls "home." Match the pushpins on these maps to the Team Facts and you will begin to see the story of the Giants unfold!

TEAM FACTS

1 East Rutherford, New Jersey—*The Giants have played here since 1976.*

2 Bryn Mawr, Pennsylvania—*Emlen Tunnell was born here.*

3 Roanoke, Virginia—*Tiki Barber was born here.*

4 Fort Bragg, North Carolina—*Joe Morris was born here.*

5 Cuthbert, Georgia—*Rosey Grier was born here.*

6 Owosso, Michigan—*Brad Van Pelt was born here.*

7 Houston, Texas—*Michael Strahan was born here.*

8 Ada, Oklahoma—*Jeremy Shockey was born here.*

9 Berkeley, California—*Amani Toomer was born here.*

10 Santa Monica, California—*Frank Gifford was born here.*

11 Budapest, Hungary—*Pete Gogolak was born here.*

12 London, England—*Osi Umenyiora was born here.*

Emlen Tunnell

Play Ball

Football is a sport played by two teams on a field that is 100 yards long. The game is divided into four 15-minute quarters. Each team must have 11 players on the field at all times. The group that has the ball is called the offense. The group trying to keep the offense from moving the ball forward is called the defense.

A football game is made up of a series of "plays." Each play starts and ends with a referee's signal. A play begins when the center snaps the ball between his legs to the quarterback. The quarterback then gives the ball to a teammate, throws (or "passes") the ball to a teammate, or runs with the ball himself. The job of the defense is to tackle the player with the ball or stop the quarterback's pass. A play ends when the ball (or player holding the ball) is "down." The offense must move the ball forward at least 10 yards every four downs. If it fails to do so, the other team is given the ball. If the offense has not made 10 yards after three downs—and does not want to risk losing the ball—it can kick (or "punt") the ball to make the other team start from its own end of the field.

At each end of a football field is a goal line, which divides the field from the end zone. A team must run or pass the ball over the goal line to score a touchdown, which counts for six points. After scoring a touchdown, a team can try a short kick for one "extra point," or try again to run or pass across the goal line for two points. Teams can score three points from anywhere on the field by kicking the ball between the goal posts. This is called a field goal.

The defense can score two points if it tackles a player while he is in his own end zone. This is called a safety. The defense can also score points by taking the ball away from the offense and crossing the opposite goal line for a touchdown. The team with the most points after 60 minutes is the winner.

Football may seem like a very hard game to understand, but the more you play and watch football, the more "little things" you are likely to notice. The next time you are at a game, look for these plays:

PLAY LIST

BLITZ—A play where the defense sends extra tacklers after the quarterback. If the quarterback sees a blitz coming, he passes the ball quickly. If he does not, he can end up at the bottom of a very big pile!

DRAW—A play where the offense pretends it will pass the ball, and then gives it to a running back. If the offense can "draw" the defense to the quarterback and his receivers, the running back should have lots of room to run.

FLY PATTERN—A play where a team's fastest receiver is told to "fly" past the defensive backs for a long pass. Many long touchdowns are scored on this play.

SQUIB KICK—A play where the ball is kicked a short distance on purpose. A squib kick is used when the team kicking off does not want the other team's fastest player to catch the ball and run with it.

SWEEP—A play where the ball carrier follows a group of teammates moving sideways to "sweep" the defense out of the way. A good sweep gives the runner a chance to gain a lot of yards before he is tackled or forced out of bounds.

Glossary

FOOTBALL WORDS TO KNOW

ALL-PRO—An honor given to the best players at their position at the end of each season.

BENCHED—Removed from the game.

BLOCK—Use the body to protect the ball carrier.

DRAFTED—Chosen from a group of the best college players. The NFL draft is held each spring.

EASTERN DIVISION—A group of teams that play in the eastern part of the country. The Giants play in the NFC East.

FIELD GOAL—A goal from the field, kicked over the crossbar and between the goal posts. A field goal is worth three points.

FUMBLE—A ball that is dropped by the player carrying it.

LINEMEN—Players who begin each down crouched at the line of scrimmage.

MOST VALUABLE PLAYER (MVP)—The award given each year to the league's best player; also given to the best player in the Super Bowl and Pro Bowl.

NATIONAL FOOTBALL CONFERENCE (NFC)—One of two groups of teams that make up the National Football League. The winner of the NFC plays the winner of the American Football Conference (AFC) in the Super Bowl.

NATIONAL FOOTBALL LEAGUE (NFL)—The league that started in 1920 and is still operating today.

NFL CHAMPIONSHIP—The game played to decide the winner of the league each year from 1933 to 1969.

NFL DRAFT—The annual meeting at which teams take turns choosing the best players in college.

NOSE TACKLE—The player in the middle of a three-man or five-man defensive line.

OVERTIME—The extra period played when a game is tied after 60 minutes.

PLAYBOOK—A group of diagrams used by a team during a season or game.

PLAYOFFS—The games played after the season to determine which teams play in the Super Bowl.

PRO BOWL—The NFL's all-star game, played after the Super Bowl.

PROFESSIONAL—A player or team that plays a sport for money. College players are not paid, so they are considered "amateurs."

SEASON TICKETS—Packages of tickets for each home game.

SUPER BOWL—The championship of football, played between the winners of the NFC and AFC.

TOTAL YARDS—Rushing yards plus receiving yards.

VETERANS—Players with great experience.

OTHER WORDS TO KNOW

ANCHORED—Held steady.

ASSASSINATED—Killed for political reasons.

BRUTALIZED—Treated very harshly.

CHERISHED—Showed deep affection for.

CLASSIC—Popular for a long time.

DEAFENING—So loud that it is difficult to hear.

DECADES—Periods of 10 years, or specific periods, such as the 1950s or 1960s.

DOMINATED—Completely controlled through the use of power.

LOGO—A symbol or design that represents a company or team.

RENOVATED—Fixed and made more modern.

SPORTS PROMOTER—A person who stages sports events.

TAILBONE—The bone that protects the base of the spine.

TRADITION—A belief or custom that is handed down from generation to generation.

VERSATILE—Able to do many things well.

Places to Go

ON THE ROAD

NEW YORK GIANTS
Giants Stadium
East Rutherford, New Jersey 07073
(201) 935-8111

THE PRO FOOTBALL HALL OF FAME
2121 George Halas Drive NW
Canton, Ohio 44708
(330) 456-8207

ON THE WEB

THE NATIONAL FOOTBALL LEAGUE   www.nfl.com
  • *Learn more about the National Football League*

THE NEW YORK GIANTS   www.giants.com
  • *Learn more about the New York Giants*

THE PRO FOOTBALL HALL OF FAME   www.profootballhof.com
  • *Learn more about football's greatest players*

ON THE BOOKSHELF

To learn more about the sport of football, look for these books at your library or bookstore:

  • Fleder, Rob–Editor. *The Football Book*. New York, NY: Sports Illustrated Books, 2005.

  • Kennedy, Mike. *Football*. Danbury, CT: Franklin Watts, 2003.

  • Savage, Jeff. *Play by Play Football*. Minneapolis, MN: Lerner Sports, 2004.

Index

PAGE NUMBERS IN **BOLD** REFER TO ILLUSTRATIONS.

The Team

MARK STEWART has written more than 20 books on football, and over 100 sports books for kids. He grew up in New York City during the 1960s rooting for the Giants and Jets, and now takes his two daughters, Mariah and Rachel, to watch them play in their home state of New Jersey. Mark comes from a family of writers. His grandfather was Sunday Editor of *The New York Times* and his mother was Articles Editor of *The Ladies' Home Journal* and *McCall's*. Mark has profiled hundreds of athletes over the last 20 years. He has also written several books about New York and New Jersey. Mark is a graduate of Duke University, with a degree in History. He lives with his daughters and wife Sarah overlooking Sandy Hook, New Jersey.

JASON AIKENS is the Collections Curator at the Pro Football Hall of Fame. He is responsible for the preservation of the Pro Football Hall of Fame's collection of artifacts and memorabilia and obtaining new donations of memorabilia from current players and NFL teams. Jason has a Bachelor of Arts in History from Michigan State University and a Master's in History from Western Michigan University where he concentrated on sports history. Jason has been working for the Pro Football Hall of Fame since 1997; before that he was an intern at the College Football Hall of Fame. Jason's family has roots in California and has been following the St. Louis Rams since their days in Los Angeles, California. He lives with his wife Cynthia and recent addition to the team Angelina in Canton, Ohio.